WILDLIFE WATCHER GUIDE

By wildlife photographers
Michael Leach and Meriel Lland

FIREFLY BOOKS

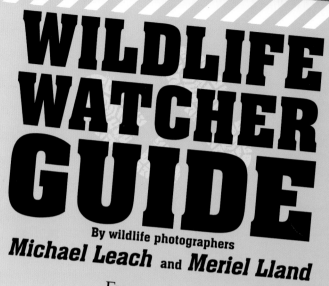

A FIREFLY BOOK

Published by Firefly Books Ltd. 2016

Copyright © 2016 Marshall Editions

First printing

Publisher Cataloging-in-Publication Data (U.S.)

CIP data for this title is available from the Library of Congress

Library and Archives Canada Cataloguing in Publication

CIP data for this title is available from Library and Archives Canada

Published in the United States by Firefly Books (U.S.) Inc. P.O. Box 1338, Ellicott Station Buffalo, New York 14205

Published in Canada by Firefly Books Ltd. 50 Staples Avenue, Unit 1 Richmond Hill, Ontario L4B 0A7

Printed and bound in China

Conceived by Marshall Editions
Publisher: Maxime Boucknooghe
Art Director: Susi Martin
Editorial Director: Laura Knowles
Production: Nikki Ingram

Designed, edited and picture researched by:
Starry Dog Books Ltd

CONTENTS

INTRODUCTION

It's a wild world out there! Today planet Earth is home to about 10,000 species of birds and 5,000 species of mammals. Some are brightly colored and stand out easily. Others can be tricky to spot — they may move fast, or be slow but well-camouflaged. Some species are rare, so finding them is a challenge.

Freeze! A hare's eyes are on the sides of its head, so it can see anything that moves to its left or right.

If you love animals, you'll want to know where and when to look for them in the wild. That's where this book comes in! It'll show you how to read the clues that animals leave in the landscape, so you can get close. You'll learn vital explorer skills, discover exciting creatures and find plenty of ideas to help you set out on wildlife adventures of your own!

PREPARE TO EXPLORE!

For great wildlife adventures, active nature explorers need fieldcraft know-how and patience. You must know where to look for animals, how to read the clues and how not to frighten them.

ESSENTIAL GEAR

You'll need cunning to get close to shy animals. Wear comfortable clothes that help you to blend in with the environment.

Use binoculars (binocs) to help you find and study wildlife from a safe distance.

THE PERFECT BACKPACK

A lightweight backpack will keep you and your gear safe.

Think comfort — you'll be wearing your backpack for long periods.

Think ease of access — you'll need to reach in to get your binoculars, camera, notebook or water bottle with minimum noise and movement.

Think hard-wearing — the pack needs to keep your gear safe and dry in all weather.

NOTEBOOK

Pack a notebook and pencil so you can write about your finds, draw them and focus in on the details. **Use a small camera,** such as a smartphone camera, to help record your sightings (see page 13).

TOP TIPS

• Pack a ruler so you can measure any animal tracks you find. This will help you to identify (ID) them.

• Use your eyes all the time! Really look at the world around you.

MAKE AN ANIMAL FACTFILE

Keep a factfile about a specific animal. Jot down things you see firsthand. Include the following:

1 Best locations to see your animal.

2 What it eats.

3 Best times of day and year to spot it.

4 Any important behavior.

Your mission is: to disappear! Wildlife explorers dress to be safe, comfortable and invisible. Wild animals are very good at spotting danger, so choose clothes that blend with the environment, provide camouflage and also keep you protected from the weather.

Did you know ❓

Loose, lightweight layers of clothing have "dead-air space" between them for extra insulation.

COMFORT IS EVERYTHING

• Keep layers of clothing easily accessible in your backpack, and add or remove layers as you need. Layered clothing helps to keep you warm and dry (see pages 70–71).

• Keep clothing flexible and easy to wear. Loose clothing allows you to move with ease.

• Wear boots with ankle support, deep-tread soles, a breathable liner and waterproof uppers. Look after them — you may be wearing them for hours!

11

TOP TIPS

• Buy boots half a size too big to allow for extra socks, which help to prevent blisters.

• Animals have great hearing so clothes need to be rustle-free, especially waterproof outer layers.

Desert camouflage for sand

Khaki camouflage for green landscapes

Winter camouflage for snow

Wear clothes that provide camouflage.

ESSENTIALS

Make sure you always carry:

A winter hat or sunhat — to keep you warm or cool and to help disguise the shine of your hair and your human outline.

Sunscreen — useful even on cloudy days.

Sunglasses — to protect your eyes.

The two most useful pieces of technology you can carry are a pair of binoculars and a smartphone. You can add macro, telephoto or extreme wide-angle lenses to a smartphone so you can take close-up, long-distance or wide photos, and you can even use it as a microscope.

TOP TIP
Look through the wrong end of your binocs for an emergency magnifier.

UNDERSTAND YOUR BINOCS

Each pair of binoculars has a name, such as 10 x 50. The first number is the magnification, so 10 x 50s make distant objects look 10 times bigger. The second number is the size of the front lens. For all-around wildlife viewing, 8 x 35 is a good choice.

PHOTO-EDITING

At home, you can upload smartphone photos to a computer and edit them using photo-edit apps.

SPOTTING SCOPE

A spotting scope is a small telescope supported on a tripod. Scopes are used to pick out detail. Some have just one magnification, others can zoom. For most wildlife watchers, x20 magnification is about right.

Attaching a smartphone camera to a spotting scope is called "digiscoping." It allows you to take close-up shots of distant animals.

FIELDCRAFT

Fieldcraft gives you the skills to track stealthily, whatever the weather or terrain; to hide without being seen; and to watch patiently without giving away your position. The aim is to stay undetected by wildlife while you observe it.

Using fieldcraft techniques, this nature explorer has made himself almost invisible!

HOW TO FOCUS BINOCULARS

Don't panic if you see a blur — here's how to get your binocs into focus:

With your eye **1**

Look at an object about 20 feet (6 m) away.

Raise binocs

Put the binocs up to your eyes.

 2

4 **Focus binocs**

Look at a more distant object. To focus, turn the focusing wheel. This will make the object more or less blurry. Practice to get faster!

Start with the eyepieces too far apart. Then move the tubes up or down until the two circles line up and become one.

3 **Extend binocs**

"S" IS FOR...

... seven rules of fieldcraft that will help you to be a better tracker:

SOUND Avoid making it!

SHINE Avoid carrying shiny objects.

SMELL Animals generally have a great sense of smell, so avoid scented hygiene products.

SLOW For animals fast movement means danger, so don't move quickly.

SURVEILLANCE Binocs are perfect for watching from a distance undetected.

SHAPE Mask your shape with camouflage and keep low.

STRAIGHT LINES Most animals feel threatened by movement approaching from head-on, so take a zigzag route using cover as much as possible.

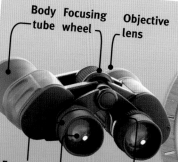

Body tube — Focusing wheel — Objective lens

Eyecup — Eyepiece lens — Adjustment ring

TOP TIP

Approach wildlife from "downwind" — when the wind is blowing from the direction of the animal toward you. This will reduce your sound and smell.

STAYING SAFE

Out in the wild, you must be prepared at all times. You never know when things may go wrong!

TOP TIP
• Keep your phone and camera in zipper-sealed bags to protect them from rain, sweat and dust.

SAFETY FIRST

Accidents can happen anywhere. To stay safe, you should:

• Always keep a mobile phone with you.

• Always tell someone where you're going.

• Explore with family or a friend. When it comes to spotting wildlife, two sets of eyes are better than one!

PONCHO

Pack a lightweight plastic poncho. It weighs almost nothing but keeps you and your gear dry in a downpour. You can even sit on it when the ground is wet.

ENERGY

Carry snacks to give you an energy boost. Flapjacks, dried fruits and cereal bars are ideal.

If you graze yourself, clean the cut and cover it to keep it clean.

FIRST AID KIT

Waterproof box
Keeps everything together and dry.

Blister bandages
Provide pain relief and prevent further blisters.

Waterproof adhesive bandages
Keep cuts and wounds clean.

Bandage
Use to wrap around sprains.

Antiseptic wipes
Use to clean wounds and stop infection.

NATURE WATCH: WOODLAND

From icy, Arctic boreal forests to steaming equatorial rainforests, woodlands are exciting habitats to explore. More than half the world's land animal species live among the trees.

There are many types of woodland made up of different kinds of trees. Deciduous, or broad-leaved, trees drop their leaves in winter. Coniferous trees, which have needle-like leaves, stay green all year. Each type of woodland attracts different wildlife.

TYPES OF WOODLAND

	Broad-leaf	Needle-leaf
Scientific name	Deciduous	Coniferous
Leaves	Lost in winter	Evergreen
Example	Oak	Fir
Food for wildlife	Insects, fruits and nuts	Cones
Wildlife	Plentiful and varied	Fewer species and more specialist

TOP TIP

Draw a tree from memory. Then draw that same tree from life. Nature explorers need to learn to look really closely!

WHO'S BEEN FEEDING?

Deciduous forests have plentiful nuts.

Mice and voles scrape the nuts with their teeth until they make a small hole, then they nibble the kernels inside.

Squirrels gnaw an opening in the nuts and break them open with their teeth.

Conifer forests produce pine cones, which are full of seeds for squirrels and mice to eat.

Mice and voles nibble cones thoroughly. The remains look tidy.

Squirrels use their strong teeth to tear into cones leaving frayed, scruffy remains.

Look closely at the signs left by animals to see who lives in the wood.

Scientists give forests special names to help us understand each habitat.

TRACKING AND SPOOR

Fieldcraft is about working with the natural environment so that you can get up close to wildlife. Here, you can find out how to track animals by reading their "spoor."

STEALTH MODE

Many animals will run away if they spot you. Use features of the landscape to mask your silhouette.

1 Watch from behind a rock to disguise your shape.

2 Sit in front of a tree or bush so your outline doesn't show up against the sky.

When tracking a fox, look out for footprints, droppings and the remains of its prey.

TOP TIPS

Animals' eyes are designed to see movement, so to avoid being spotted by an animal you are watching, keep as still as possible.

Did you know ❓

Spoor is any sign or trace left by wildlife. It includes footprints, scent, hair, broken twigs or "scat" — solid waste matter excreted by an animal.

TELLTALE SIGNS

There are several ways you can find out if animals are using a trail:

1 Place twigs across a track or hole. If an animal passes by, it will knock the twigs over, so you'll know the path is used.

2 Put some tape, sticky side outward, around a twig next to a track. The hairs of passing animals will stick to the tape. The color and texture of the hairs will help you to identify the animals.

SCAT

Hare

Look out for scat left behind by animals:

Plant-eating animals produce small, roundish droppings that they pile or scatter.

Carnivores leave single pieces of scat that often contain hair, feathers and even small bones.

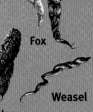

Fox

Weasel

Badger

Finding feathers can help you to identify the birds that live in a forest. Different feathers work to keep a bird warm or to help it fly.

FIELD GUIDE

Use a field guide to discover which birds live in your location. Compare the feathers you find to the illustrations.

FEATHERS

Body feathers cover the bird's head and body and keep it streamlined for flight.

Down feathers are the smallest, softest feathers. They provide extra warmth and are found beneath the tougher, exterior feathers.

Primary flight feathers are at the outer edges of the wings.

HAIR FINDS

Hair on a thin branch may be from a small animal such as a squirrel.

Animal hair often gets caught on fences and plants. Collect samples and compare the different hair colors with photos of forest animals.

A clump of red hair found low down on a tree trunk in spring probably belongs to a red fox.

Cream and black banded hair on low barbed wire comes from a badger.

Look for the different types of feathers on this eagle owl.

Semiplumes have a soft, fluffy texture like down feathers, but a well-developed shaft like body feathers. They are often found beneath the body feathers, where they help streamlining and add extra warmth.

Secondary wing feathers are on the inside of the wings.

Tail feathers can be long and decorative, or may help a bird to steer and keep its balance.

IDENTIFYING FOOTPRINTS

Walkers on soft surfaces, such as mud, sand or snow, leave footprints or tracks. Check out the handy reference on the right to find out how to ID footprints.

TRAILS

Trails are the pathways regularly used by animals. Sometimes you can figure out which animal made the track by reading the signs. For example, badgers go under obstacles, so a track that goes under a fence, with ground plants worn away, is probably a badger run!

The large, clawed feet of a North American badger sink into the snow, leaving a trail.

MAMMAL PRINTS

There are four types of mammal prints:

Sole walkers Some mammals, such as bears, walk on the soles of their feet. On each paw they have five toes, one or more palm pads and a heel pad. Many have claws.

Toe walkers Animals such as wolves and foxes walk on their toes, and are often fast runners. They leave palm prints and four or five toe and claw prints.

Hoof walkers Animals such as horses and donkeys have one toe on each foot. The toe is covered by a strong nail, or hoof. Hooves leave an almost circular print.

Cloven-hoof walkers Deer and cattle have four toes on each foot. They walk on the two middle toes. The toes are covered in tough nail, or hoof, which is split or "cloven."

Birds Most birds have four toes on each foot. A few have only three toes. Most often, bird prints show three toes pointing forward and one backward.

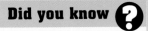

TOP TIP

To ID an animal's tracks, count the number of toes on each footprint. Are there claw or web marks? Are there pad marks? Is there a line left by the animal's tail?

Did you know ?

Foxes leave a trail that you can smell! And slugs leave a silvery trail you can follow.

BUILDING BLINDS

In the woods, you'll need a place to take cover so that you can watch animals and birds unseen. The best place to do this is inside a shelter or behind a screen. Called blinds, these hiding places are often made of camouflaged fabric, but can be made of anything that blends in with the surroundings.

NATURE RESERVES

Many nature reserves have large, comfortable hides. Some even have screens showing live footage from nest cameras!

Slimbridge Wetland Centre, England

SETTING UP YOUR BLIND

The best place to position a blind is next to a tree or bush so it's camouflaged against the leaves.

Leave the blind for a few days to let the animals get used to it. They'll soon treat it as part of their surroundings.

Place your blind so it overlooks a spot where animals go regularly, such as a pool or feeding place.

TOP TIPS

• Blinds work well with birds because most species have a poor sense of smell.

• Set up a blind near a garden bird feeder to get some amazing close-up photos.

Portable blinds are light to carry and are camouflaged for different habitats. Most of them are big enough for just one person.

Did you know ?

Vultures are one of the few birds that have a good sense of smell. They are scavengers, which means they eat animals that are already dead, and they can smell a body from over 1 mile (1.6 km) away.

If you don't have a portable blind, don't panic! There are other ways you can stay hidden from wildlife in the woods. Use whatever is at hand. Fallen branches and leafy twigs woven together can make a perfect blind.

SCRIM

Scrim is camouflage netting.
It costs very little, weighs almost nothing and you can use it to make a blind that will make you almost invisible to wildlife!

Choose the right color scrim for the habitat you are in.

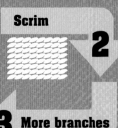

HOW TO MAKE A SCRIM BLIND

Branches **1** Find a bush with fairly low, open branches.

String a large piece of scrim across the branches and weigh down the base with some large stones.

Scrim **2**

3 **More branches** Collect thin, fallen branches with leaves attached and lean them up against the netting.

4 **Wait** Sit patiently behind the blind and wait for wildlife to appear!

SHADOW FRIGHT

Keep an eye on where your shadow falls. Small animals, especially butterflies and bugs, can be spooked if your huge shadow falls over them in sunshine.

Keep the sun in front of you, so your shadow falls behind you.

Using branches and netting, this wildlife explorer is setting up a blind in the Amazon rainforest.

Shine your flashlight in the forest after dark, and you'll probably spot strange eyes staring back at you! Nocturnal animals have a special layer at the backs of their eyes that acts like a mirror and helps them to pick up even the faintest light.

? Did you know

Some insects, such as fireflies and glowworms, communicate using lights. They have chemicals in their tails that glow bright yellow or green. Often there are hundreds of these insects in one place and the forest shines with tiny lights.

WHOSE EYES?

A deer's eyes look yellow at night.

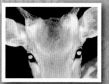

A cat's eyes appear green.

Owls' eyes glow red.

A rabbit's eyes also glow red.

RED FILTER

Nocturnal animals can see well in the dark, but most cannot see the color red. Cover the front of a flashlight with a thin sheet of red plastic and you'll be able to see at night without being seen.

This ocelot cannot see the red light.

The light in this mouse-deer's eyes is bouncing straight back toward the light source.

TOP TIP

At night, checking the height of an animal's reflecting eyes from the ground and their width apart can help to ID the animal.

Find out what

it's really like exploring

outdoors with

real-life explorers

Michael Leach

and **Meriel Lland.**

Ⓠ WHAT'S THE WORST THING ABOUT WORKING OUTDOORS?

Ⓐ *Michael: Tropical rain! In some forests it rains every day and everything gets soaked.*

Ⓐ *Meriel: Weight! Camera gear is super heavy!*

Ⓠ WHERE DO YOU SLEEP WHEN YOU'RE WORKING IN A FOREST?

Ⓐ *Michael: Depends on the forest. A hammock covered by a tarp keeps you off the ground and sheltered.*

Ⓐ *Meriel: Luxury! Sometimes you have to make do with a bivouac sack, or bivy, on the ground (see photo below).*

Ⓠ WHICH IS BEST, WORKING IN HOT OR COLD PLACES?

Ⓐ *Michael: I'm happy in both. But there is something special about the Arctic in winter. If you have the right clothes you can be really comfortable at under 15°F (-10°C). And best of all, there are no biting bugs!*

Ⓐ *Meriel: Humidity is a toughy! Give me dry desert air at 95°F (35°C) anytime! Or dry season on the Savannah.*

Q WHAT'S THE BIGGEST DANGER IN THE FOREST?

A **Michael:** In the tropics, it's definitely mosquitoes. They carry malaria, and that's a killer disease.

A **Meriel:** But mosquitoes are just the beginning. There are snakes and spiders and all kinds of creatures with fangs and suckers just waiting to find out what you taste like!

A **Michael:** And in Arctic forests it's bull moose in the breeding season. If you spot one, head for cover!

A **Meriel:** In the wrong mood, they're dangerously quick to charge.

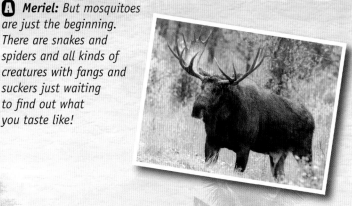

Q SO, WHAT'S THE NASTIEST BITE YOU'VE HAD?

A **Michael:** Nastiest... Bear? Python? Or maybe a mysterious underwater critter that got me in South Africa. That one had me on antibiotics.

A **Meriel:** Ouch! Mystery biters are the worst. With no ID the doctors are just guessing about treatment. The outdoors can be scary!

NATURE WATCH: GARDENS, PARKS AND CITIES

Wildlife once lived only in wild places, but not any more! Our towns and cities are full of amazing animals. Urban nature explorers can find adventure in their own neighborhoods!

Cities are growing and more animals are moving in! Mice and pigeons have lived close to humans for a long time, but now you might see badgers, rabbits, squirrels, house sparrows and even deer living in a city's green spaces.

Did you know ?

Cities are much warmer than the countryside. Cars, houses, people and factories produce heat, and this keeps temperatures up to 15°F (about 8°C) higher! The extra warmth helps animals to find food — the colder it is, the harder it is to find food.

SPOTTER'S CHECKLIST

Animals in towns can become tame because they are always surrounded by the sight, sound and scent of humans. See how many of these you can spot in your local town:

Starling

Fox

MAP OUT YOUR LOCAL PATCH

Using either a town map from a tourist office or an online satellite map, choose an area you'd like to explore for wildlife. Make sure your patch includes the older part of town, trees, water, open south-facing areas and places to watch from.

TOP TIP

Mammals can't move far in a town safely, so if you do spot a mammal, it probably lives in the area year-round. Stay alert and you may be able to track it to its home.

Rabbit

Duck

Squirrel

Goose

House sparrow

Pigeon

Look for wildlife in places where animals might find food, such as parks, ponds and gardens. Many people feed wildlife, for example with bird feeders, and animals can come to see humans as friends.

TOP TIP

Make squeaking noises by kissing the back of your hand very loudly! This can bring small birds out of shrubs and bushes.

Small birds such as this sparrow can become tame enough to feed from your hand!

Did you know ?

Birds can only digest the soft parts of a berry but not the hard seed inside. A few hours after eating, the seed comes out in the bird's droppings. Seeds can be dropped many miles from where the bird ate. Some start to grow, and this is how new trees appear all around the country.

STAKE-OUT: CITY TREES

Look out for trees that produce berries in the fall — for example holly and rowan. Birds from the countryside often move in to towns at this time of year to feed on berries in parks and gardens.

Raccoon

STAKE-OUT: TRASH CANS AND DUMPSTERS

Keep an eye on bins outside fast food restaurants and in parks and playgrounds. People throw away lots of food, and animals know exactly where to find it.

MAKING A HOME FOR WILDLIFE

Feeding wildlife in your garden "baits" the animals — it attracts them to the places you want them to be! This is what expert wildlife watchers do to get close.

BUILD A FIVE-STAR
FEEDING STATION

Choose a site away from bushes, which may conceal predators.

1

Set up a platform outside your window.

2

Attach a peanut or mixed-seed feeder.

3

Fill the feeder with nuts and seeds.

4

Watch from indoors, keeping a camera or binoculars handy.

A peacock butterfly feeds on nectar from a spring blossom.

NECTAR-FEEDER

Some hummingbirds winter in Central America and fly north to nest in the spring. Their main food is nectar. Each tiny bird eats more than twice its own body weight of nectar each day. People help the hummers by hanging nectar-feeders in their gardens.

BUTTERFLIES AND MOTHS

Butterflies, moths and their caterpillars need food, too! Grow plants with lots of nectar, such as buddleia and lavender. ID your local species and learn what food plants their caterpillars need. Plant these too!

WARNING ⚠

Safety first

Always wash your hands after filling bird feeders and cleaning bird-feeding stations.

A simple way to help bring wildlife into your garden is to provide water. For birds, drinking is just as important as eating. Providing water may help them to survive, especially in winter when pools freeze over.

A blackbird splashes water over its feathers and skin to clean them.

BUILD A BUG HOTEL

Solitary insects will make a winter home in your comfy bug hotel.

1 Fill one or more short pieces of pipe with small sticks and leaves.

2 Hide the pipes somewhere out of sight.

3 Ladybugs, lacewings and other insects will shelter and even hibernate inside.

Ladybug

Lacewing

Did you know ?

Some bats will nest in boxes. Find out which species live locally and put up boxes that are designed just for them.

NEST-BOXES

Check which birds live nearby and put up suitable nest-boxes.

1 Small garden birds, such as chickadees, need a nest-box hole measuring 1 inch (2.5 cm) across. Larger birds, such as starlings, need a hole 1.75 inches (4.5 cm) wide.

2 To prevent chicks falling out, and to keep them safe from cats, the hole needs to be 5 inches (12.5 cm) above the nest-box floor.

3 Attach the nest-box to a wall or tree at a height of at least 6.5 feet (2 m) above the ground.

Leave a pile of twigs in the garden for birds to sleep in at night.

WARNING ⚠

Safety first
• Always get an adult to help you site nest-boxes.
• Wear gloves when you clean out nest-boxes before spring each year.

SET UP A GARDEN WEBCAM

If you're tech-savvy, try setting up a webcam in your garden so you can see who's busy after dark.

TOP TIPS

• Focus webcams on feeding platforms and bird baths.

• Take your trailcam with you on vacation so you can explore new habitats.

TRAILCAMS

Weatherproof and motion-activated, trailcams capture photos, videos and sound, by day and night. They record to an SD card, so you can view the recordings on your computer and share or print the images.

Trailcam

Pine marten on a garden fence, filmed by a trailcam

NEST-BOX CAMS

A nest-box cam can be wired or wireless. The best ones record color images by day and infrared (IR) black-and-white images by night. A microphone picks up sounds. Unlike trailcams, nest-box cams do require some knowledge of electronics, so seek advice from a recognized supplier.

Blue tit feeding her chicks

A European badger is caught on webcam crossing a home's lawn at night.

Find out what

it's really like exploring

urban habitats

with real-life nature explorers

Michael Leach
and Meriel Lland.

Q **WHAT'S THE MOST EXCITING ANIMAL YOU'VE FILMED IN A CITY?**

A *Michael: No question. Kestrels. They were the first falcons in the world to move to cities. In wild places they nest on cliffs, but now you can see them nesting on skyscrapers and high bridges.*

A *Meriel: Musk ox in Greenland maybe? But I'm not sure Kangerlussuaq counts as a city! I'll go for red foxes. They're brilliant survivors and experts at city life. They're useful too — they keep down the number of rats and mice.*

A *Michael: Absolutely, plus they've learned to raid trash cans and take food off bird-feeding platforms at night.*

Kestrel

Barn owl

Q SO WHAT MAKES CITY WILDLIFE SO SPECIAL?

A *Meriel: City wildlife changes all the time.*

A *Michael: Yes, new animals move in and change their behavior.*

A *Meriel: That makes it exciting.*

A *Michael: A few years ago, foxes kept clear of towns. Now, they wander the streets in broad daylight. The number of ring-necked parakeets is growing and a lot are living in cities.*

A *Meriel: It's a good time to be a city wildlife spotter.*

A *Michael: Now you don't have to drive miles to see animals.*

A *Meriel: Which is great! It's good for people too — it's wonderful to go for a walk in a park and see squirrels and ducks and geese.*

A *Michael: Humans are part of the natural world too...*

A *Meriel: Exactly! And seeing animals makes a day better.*

Red fox

Kestrel feeding her chicks

NATURE WATCH: WATERY WORLDS

Much of our watery world is still unexplored, so it's a great place for wildlife watchers to make discoveries. Our oceans, lakes, ponds and rivers are home to some amazing wildlife.

WILDLIFE TO LOOK OUT FOR

The margins where water and land meet are exciting places to watch for animals. You can also take a boat trip for an exciting wildlife adventure!

LOOK OUT FOR THESE

1 From beaches and coastal rocks, you may spot these saltwater animals:

Starfish

Crab

Dolphin

Seal

2 From the shores of ponds and streams, look out for freshwater animals, such as:

Dragonfly

Frog

Beaver

Toad

Dolphins may swim close to your boat to take a look at you!

BEAVERS

Beavers build their lodges (homes) from branches. They protect their lodges from predators by building dams, using trees that they fell with their teeth. Lie low near a beaver lodge at around sunset and you may be lucky enough to spot beavers foraging on land.

Dam

Lodge

Beaver

Dragonfly larva

Did you know

Dragonfly larvae are one of the deadliest hunters. They eat almost anything, including fish. Some larvae stay in a pond for five years before they turn into dragonflies.

POND-DIPPING

There's a hidden world of fascinating wildlife just under the surface of freshwater ponds. You can hunt some amazing mini-beasts on a pond-dipping safari. Just dip in for a closer look...

POND-DIPPING
HERE'S WHAT TO DO:

Fill a tray with pond water to make a temporary home for the animals you'll catch.

PREPARE 1

HUNT 2

Slowly and gently, sweep a net around in circles in the pond.

When the safari is over, gently put the mini-beasts back into the pond.

Download online guides to identify your mini-beasts.

7 **RETURN**

 6 **IDENTIFY**

TOP TIP

Dip at the water's edge and around plants— creatures hide there to escape predators.

FIND **3**

Empty the net into the tray.

GET CLOSE

Use a magnifier to study the strange beasts you've caught.

4

Photograph or video your finds and make notes.

5 **RECORD**

WARNING ⚠

Safety first

Keep away from deep water — the best beasts live in the shallows. Always wash your hands at the end of a mini-beast hunt.

Getting up close to birds and animals that live in wetlands or on open water can be difficult, so these are great places to use binocs or a spotting scope.

HOW TO SCOUT WITH BINOCS

On open water, use binocs to scan or "scout" the horizon for movements. First, make sure your binocs are in focus (see page 14). Then...

1 ...**breathe slowly and evenly.** Tiny movements of your hands can make it tricky to focus. Taking gentle breaths will make it easier to keep your hands steady.

2 **Choose the area** you want to explore, then slowly move the binocs over the scene from left to right and back again. Don't jump from area to area. Look for movement or distinctive colors or shapes.

Binocs are especially useful for whale watching.

TRIPOD

A tripod is an essential bit of gear for keeping your scope steady. Carry a tripod with the scope already attached so you are ready to spot.

Oystercatchers and other wading birds feed on small creatures that live just under the surface of mud. They pick them out with their long bills.

GOLDEN RULES FOR SCOUTING

1 Scan with your naked eye for close movements.

2 Scan a bit farther out with binocs.

3 Switch to a scope and zoom in on likely areas.

Sand and mud are a spoor detective's dream because they often show clear prints. You can have fun finding out who recently left the scene by identifying the tracks!

FROG
PRINTS

Amphibians, such as frogs, toads and newts, begin their lives in water, and as adults generally live close to water to stop their skin drying out. This means you can often find their prints in the mud near ponds and streams.

Footprints left by a frog leaping

Trail left by a frog walking

After eating, seals leave the water and come onto dry land to rest, making tracks with their tail and front flippers.

WATER BIRD
PRINTS
· · · · · · · · · · · · · · · · ·

Most water birds have three forward-facing toes joined by webbing. Webbed feet are good for paddling.

Gull

Duck

Goose

Coot

Coots have three very long, forward-facing toes edged with lobes of skin that expand or contract when the bird swims.

Did you know ❓

Otters spend much of their time in water. Some live in freshwater rivers and marshes; others live beside the sea. Like water birds, otters also have webbed feet. They mark their territory with smelly droppings called spraint, which they leave on rocks and riverbanks.

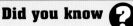

TIDE-POOLING

If you scramble over the rocks at low tide, you're likely to find a tide pool holding hidden treasures! For a few hours, marine creatures get caught in these pools. Then, when the tide comes back in, the creatures swim free.

TOP TIPS

On a sunny day, wear polarizing sunglasses. These will cut down the surface reflections on the water so you can see farther into the tide pool.

AQUASCOPE

Use an aquascope to see below the surface of the water. Push the wide end, which holds a clear plastic lens, into the water and look through the eyepiece. The cone cuts out surface reflection, giving a clear view of what lies under the water.

SPOTTER'S GUIDE

Some amazing animals lie in tide pools waiting for the sea to return. How many of these have you seen?

Mussels

Sea urchin

DO'S AND DON'TS

· · · · · · · · · · · · · · · · ·

• Do make sure you face the sea in case of sudden waves.

• Don't touch or disturb your finds! If you move a piece of seaweed or a rock to see a creature more clearly, make sure you replace it.

• Do ID and photograph your finds!

Barnacles

Starfish

Hermit crab

Anemone

Find out what

it's really like exploring for wildlife in **dangerous places** with real-life explorers **Michael Leach** and **Meriel Lland.**

Q THE ARCTIC COMBINES THE DANGERS OF A WATERY AND AN ICY WORLD. WHAT'S THE BIGGEST DANGER YOU FACED THERE?

A *Michael: In the Arctic, I guess it's bears.*

A *Meriel: Polar bears have to be treated with respect.*

A *Michael: They are the only mammal to see people as a normal part of their diet!*

A *Meriel: And ice melt is making them even hungrier.*

Q HAVE YOU EVER BEEN IN A LIFE OR DEATH SITUATION?

A *Michael:* I've had a few close calls with teeth and antlers and icy roads. I got caught in a hurricane a few years ago. Our entire camp — tent, food and equipment — was taken by the wind.

Q WHAT ARE THE REAL DANGERS OF WORKING IN THE WILD?

A *Michael:* Accidents and illness.

A *Meriel:* Being injured or sick miles away from help.

A *Michael:* Scary! You need a good first aid kit...

A *Meriel:* ...and you need to know how to use it.

Q DO YOU EVER GET SCARED?

A *Meriel:* All the time. But that's healthy. Fear keeps you alive!

A *Michael:* Exactly! I once accidentally trod on a crocodile's tail in Kenya. I'm not sure which one of us was the most surprised, but I was certainly the most frightened.

NATURE WATCH: MOUNTAINS AND HIGH COUNTRY

Exploring high country will test your endurance. The weather can turn from sunshine to snow in a matter of moments. But spotting the amazing wildlife will make the hike worthwhile!

Mountains are home to some of the world's rarest animals — giant pandas, mountain gorillas and snow leopards all live in high, remote places. But closer to home, there are plenty of other species to spot.

LOOK OUT
FOR THESE

Depending on your location, you may be able to spot these high country animals:

Golden eagle

Peregrine falcon

Mountain hare

Wild goat

Goat antelope

FLYING HIGH

Kestrel

Eagle

Osprey

Kite

Falcon

Birds of prey are powerful predators. They have hooked beaks for tearing flesh and curved claws called talons. To identify them in flight, you need to look at their size and silhouette.

Agile and hardy, mountain goats can climb up bare rock.

STAIRS

A great way to improve fitness in readiness for treks in high country is to train on stairs! Begin by fast-walking up a flight of stairs three times, then walk on the spot for a minute. Increase your workout weekly until you can do this ten times.

CAMOUFLAGE AND BLINDS

In high country, you are likely to find yourself out in the open with nowhere to hide. To avoid being spotted by animals, you'll need to learn some special skills for staying concealed.

GHILLIE SUIT

On mountains, where blinds are tricky to use because of high winds, some wildlife watchers wear ghillie suits. These are made of long, ragged pieces of camouflaged cloth made to look like leaves and twigs.

HOW TO HIDE IN OPEN COUNTRY

Smell
Especially important in the hills, always walk with the wind blowing in your face; your scent will be blown away from the target animal ahead of you.

Shape
Don't walk on the brow of a hill — animals will soon spot your outline against the sky. Move below the skyline and keep low against the hillside.

Cover
When stalking in high country, hide behind rocks and shrubs to scan an area. This is called "finding cover."

The "army crawl," used by soldiers, allows you to move forward stealthily on elbows, knees and toes, keeping very low to the ground.

• Practice army crawling at home to build up strength.

• No ghillie suit? Roll a length of camo netting around yourself instead!

in hill country, the temperature drops about 3 to 4°F (2°C) for every 1,000 ft (300 m) you climb. It's important to be prepared for bad weather. If things go wrong, you may be in the hills for longer than you intended.

EMERGENCY KIT:

In case of emergencies, always carry the following items:

• **Lightweight plastic or foil survival bag** — these are wind and waterproof, and will help you retain heat.

• **Warm hat**
• **Headlamp**
• **Whistle** — to attract attention if you're in trouble
• **High-visibility vest**
• **Extra food**
• **Water**
• **Map**

• **GPS** — most smartphones have GPS apps and maps, some for free
• **Compass** — to find out how to use one, follow the link on page 93

Foil survival bag

LAYERS

To enjoy the mountains, you need to know how to dress. Modern hiking gear is designed to be worn in layers. It can prevent overheating when you are on the move, but will keep you warm when you stop.

Four layers of clothing

Choose a headlamp with large buttons that you can press while wearing gloves.

TOP TIP

Wear two pairs of gloves: an inner cotton liner, great for keeping hands warm while you are writing, and an outer insulating pair.

READING THE LANDSCAPE

Mountain species are not always easy to find. Check out the greener parts of a hill. Green means good plants to eat, and wild animals are never far from their food. Gray hillsides are rocky, with fewer animals.

TOP TIP

Walk slowly when scanning for wildlife in snow. Lots of mountain animals turn white in winter, making them difficult to spot.

PATHWAYS AND
TRACKS

Over time, animal trails develop, crossing open landscape. Follow well-worn paths whenever you can. The trails often provide the easiest walking for both wildlife and humans. Birds and small animals frequently feed around these tracks, too.

Hare

Roe deer

ANIMALS GET
THIRSTY

Water is hard to find in the mountains because rain runs downhill. If you discover a pool or stream, stop and watch for a while. Wildlife often come to drink and bathe.

Moose drinking

Look for wildlife on south-facing slopes. The north sides of mountains don't get as much sunlight and are usually colder.

Did you know ?

Ravens are one of the few birds that like windy days. They seem to play in storms, flying upside down and even backward!

Find out which items of technology are the most useful to real-life explorers Michael Leach and Meriel Lland.

Q WHAT ARE YOUR TOP TECH TIPS FOR WILDLIFE PHOTOGRAPHY?

A Michael: *Trailcams are great for shy animals...*

A Meriel: *...and to stake out remote locations.*

A Michael: *You get a photo of the animal undisturbed by people.*

A Meriel: *That's so important. We get the same kind of "secret" shots using a thermal-imaging camera at night.*

A Michael: *The animals give out heat, which our gear records.*

A Meriel: *We can watch their behavior in complete darkness...*

A Michael: *...and the animals stay undisturbed.*

(Q) IS IT SAFE TO USE DRONES TO FILM WILDLIFE?

(A) **Meriel:** *Drones let you film things from amazing new angles.*

(A) **Michael:** *They're perfect for looking down on big species, such as elephants or polar bears.*

(A) **Meriel:** *But you have to be careful.*

(A) **Michael:** *A drone can look very much like a bird of prey to some smaller animals.*

(A) **Meriel:** *If they come too close, they can cause panic. Animal welfare always comes first.*

(Q) WHAT TECHNOLOGY DO YOU USE ON LONG EXPEDITIONS TO WILD PLACES?

(A) **Meriel:** *The big game-changer for me was the smartphone. It gave us a library, a compass, maps, GPS and an emergency communication system.*

(A) **Michael:** *But lots of the places we work have no mobile phone service, so for emergency communication we take a satellite phone.*

(A) **Meriel:** *The signal from a satellite phone goes straight up to a satellite at the edge of space. Sat-phones can be used anywhere on Earth...*

(A) **Michael:** *...with the help of solar chargers. Portable solar panels don't produce enough power to watch TV, but they are perfect for charging phones and camera batteries, essential in the wilderness!*

NATURE WATCH:
MEADOW,
FARMLAND AND
DRY LANDS

Take a walk along farmland footpaths and you can spot a huge range of creatures, especially along hedgerows and on the rough grass at the edges of fields, next to crops.

Farmed land and grassland produce much of the food that we eat, but they can also teem with wildlife.

Did you know ?

• There are nearly 50 species of deer. Each species has differently shaped antlers. Male deer use their antlers for fighting. They keep them for a few months, then they drop and a little later new ones start to grow.

• Dropped antlers are eaten by mice, squirrels and rabbits. Look carefully and you can see their teeth marks!

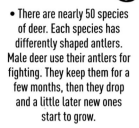

LOOK OUT FOR THESE

Rabbit

Roe deer

Hare

Crow

In winter, huge flocks of up to 10,000 birds gather on fields to search for seeds. Sandhill cranes have flocked to this corn field in New Mexico, United States.

COUNTRY CODE

Explore farmland carefully and with respect for the people who live and work there. Follow this guide:

Enjoy the countryside and respect its life and work

Use gates and stiles to cross hedges and walls

Guard against risk of fire

Leave gates as you find them

Be safe — plan ahead

Keep pets under control

Take your litter home

Consider other people

Take special care on country roads

Leave livestock, crops and machinery alone

Don't make unnecessary noise

Protect wildlife, plants and trees

Keep to public paths across farmland

Care for the environment

COLD-BLOODED CREATURES

Reptiles love open country, where prey is plentiful. Small lizards eat flies and crickets, and most snakes hunt small mammals, such as mice.

TOP TIP
Use a field guide to identify the snakes that live in your area.

If a lizard is attacked, it can break off its own tail and then grow a new one, as this lizard has done. The predator goes off with the tail and the lizard escapes.

This grass snake is basking in the sun to warm up its blood.

TRACKING SNAKES

1 Snakes are cold-blooded, which means their body temperature is dependent on the temperature of their surroundings. Look for them first thing in the morning, when they bask in sunlight to warm up.

2 Snakes judge the size of approaching animals by feeling the vibrations their feet make. If you stamp your feet, the snake will think you are BIG and it's unlikely to attack.

3 Never touch snakes! Only 600 of the 3,000 species are venomous, but they can all bite!

4 Take care around fallen logs or boulders in case a snake is resting there. Keep your hands and feet out of areas you can't see.

Did you know

Snake skin doesn't stretch as the snake grows, so every few weeks a snake sheds its old skin. Underneath is a new, bigger skin, with exactly the same markings. If you are lucky, you may find bits of shed snake skin.

Meadows are home to numerous butterfly and moth species. Butterflies love sunshine and hate high winds, so look for them in sheltered places with flowers, where they can settle to eat.

You can tell these are butterflies and not moths because their antennae are club-shaped. A moth's antennae look like feathers (see Night Light box on opposite page).

BUTTERFLY WATCHING

1 Butterfly species are active at different times of day, so to see different species, check the same area in the morning, mid day and late afternoon.

2 Some butterflies don't move when a person gets close, but others fly immediately, so use binoculars and watch them from a distance.

TOP TIP

If you see a hairy caterpillar, don't touch it! Some species protect themselves from predators with stinging hairs that could give you a rash.

NIGHT LIGHT

After dark on a summer evening, leave a ground-floor light on and windows closed. Moths will be attracted to the light and will land on the windowpane. Go outside and see if you can ID the visiting moths.

Small mammals such as weasels, voles and harvest mice are shy and difficult to spot. The best way to see them is to sit quietly at the edge of a field, where the animals have more cover from predators and more food sources.

Tiny harvest mice, weighing less than 1/5 ounce (about 5 g), live in meadows and reed beds. Look for their grass nests (about the size of a tennis ball), where they sleep and have their babies.

STALKING HARES AND RABBITS

Hares and rabbits have eyes on the sides of their heads, so they can see enemies coming from all around. Unlike with most wildlife, it's best to get close to them by approaching slowly from directly in front.

BAT DETECTOR

Bats are small flying mammals. They use ultrasound — a system of squeaking and listening to the echoes — to navigate and find prey. A bat detector picks up the bats' sounds, which are too high-pitched for many people to hear, and turns them into lower noises that can be used to ID the bats.

Frequency kHz

Digital Precision

BAITING THE HUNTERS

When frightened or surprised, many small mammals produce a short squeak. If you softly suck the back of your hand, with practice you can make the same sound. This may attract predators, such as weasels, who come to investigate.

Find out what

it's really like exploring

farmland for wildlife

with real-life nature explorers

Michael Leach
and **Meriel Lland.**

[Q] WHAT ARE YOUR FAVORITE ANIMALS TO PHOTOGRAPH ON FARMLAND?

[A] *Michael:* Farmland's fantastic for birds.

[A] *Meriel:* Where there are cows and sheep and horses, there'll be bugs...

[A] *Michael:* ...and where there are bugs, there'll be birds!

[A] *Meriel:* Great to check out plowing time, too.

[A] *Michael:* Plows turn the soil over and bring up worms and grubs.

[A] *Meriel:* Hundreds of birds can gather to grab the food — very dramatic!

Q WHAT ARE THE BEST TIMES TO EXPLORE FARMLAND?

A *Michael:* In spring we stake out puddles and mud patches.

A *Meriel:* Birds such as swallows and thrushes use mud to make their nests.

A *Michael:* Once they find good building material they'll keep coming back!

A *Meriel:* And harvest-time is great for flocks. Crops such as wheat and barley bring the birds down to the seeds left in fields.

Q WHAT FARMLAND SPECIES DO YOU ENJOY WORKING WITH THE MOST?

A *Michael:* Owls. No question. Find an owl pellet and you can start to understand its whole habitat.

A *Meriel:* With the help of a little pellet dissection?

A *Michael:* Definitely! You see, most owls swallow their food in one gulp, and a few hours later they cough up a pellet. The pellet contains hairs, bones and teeth from their last meal.

A *Meriel:* All the bits they can't digest.

A *Michael:* Exactly, and the pellet gives us clues about the identity of the small animals in the area.

A *Meriel:* Remember dissecting pellets in Kenya?

A *Michael:* Kept us busy for weeks.

SHARING
WILDLIFE SPOTTING

Watching wildlife is lots of fun on your own, with friends and family or in much bigger groups. Sharing your discoveries helps scientists to build up a picture of what's happening to our wildlife.

REMOTE WILDLIFE VIEWING

Active nature explorers around the world share their wildlife sightings by setting up cameras and streaming images on the Internet. From your laptop, you can spot parrots in the rainforest, explore kelp forests under the ocean or check out the action at an African waterhole.

TOP TIPS

It might be afternoon in your time zone, but night time on the other side of the world. Check the time difference and visit live-cam sites when the animals are active.

WEBSITES

Open a window onto international wildlife watching by exploring the breathtaking live nature-cam network. The animal behavior you see online will really help you to understand the wildlife in your own area.

www.montereybayaquarium.org
www.simonkingwildlife.com
www.wildlifekate.co.uk

www.explore.org
www.wildearth.tv
www.africam.com

ZOO CAMS

Zoos, rehabilitation centers and animal parks have live-cam feeds. Meet chimps and gorillas, study tiger behavior, watch leaf-cutter ants, penguins and giraffes.

Zoo-cam in a chimp enclosure.

Below: A tiger peers into a remote camera.

Nature explorers in Hawaii share their sightings on the Internet.

Blogs are a great way to share nature discoveries. Try making a blog of your own, featuring your own patch — the area where you explore. You could make it an online field guide to your local park, route to school or your own back yard.

PRINTED GOODS

Lots of online suppliers offer unique photobooks made using your own photos and words, which you upload from your computer. Your book could be a collection of all the species you've spotted in your life, along with your field notes. You can also have your wildlife photos printed onto mugs, T-shirts, bags or cushions, to give as gifts.

LINKS

These websites contain useful information:

Sites involved with active conservation:
Ispot — www.ispotnature.org
Defenders of wildlife — www.defenders.org
Wildlife Trust — www.wildlifetrusts.org

Sites to help you ID and find info:
youngbirders.aba.org
www.first-nature.com

CREATE A BLOG

On a blog, you can share photos, videos, sound, drawings and stories of your sightings. Most social media sites need you to be over 13 to set up a blog, so if you are younger, partner with a parent who can help you to get started and stay safe.

For spotting-sheets on almost anything:
www.wildlifewatch.org.uk/spotting-sheets

For how to use a compass:
www.discovertheforest.org/what-to-do/

Tide-pooling ID chart:
www.mcsuk.org/downloads/mcs/MCS_seashore_safari_guide.pdf

For guidance on setting up a blog:
www.kidslearntoblog.com

For information on tracks and spoor:
www.naturetracking.com

Amphibians animals that live part of their lives in water and part on land.

Blind a screen to hide behind, or a camouflaged shelter to hide inside, when you are watching an animal. It hides you and your equipment from the target animal.

Carnivore an animal that eats meat.

Cold-blooded having a body temperature that is regulated by the environment.

Habitat an animal or plant's type of home. The place where it finds food, shelter and a mate.

ID short for "identification."

Nocturnal an animal that comes out at night.

Pellet a ball of matter, for example bones and fur, that some birds regurgitate, or bring back into their mouths, from their stomachs after swallowing but not digesting the material.

Scan to survey an area.

Scat droppings or feces.

Scrim lightweight, camouflaged netting used to cover a hide.

Scout to look for an animal or signs of an animal.

Spoor may include tracks, scents, scat or damaged foliage. Finding spoor helps to locate and identify animals.

Spraint the droppings or dung of an otter.

Trailcam an automatic camera that fires when an animal appears, also known as a camera-trap.

Warm-blooded an animal that is able to regulate, or control, its own body temperature.

ACKNOWLEDGMENTS

About the Authors

Michael Leach is a professional wildlife photographer and author. He is fascinated by animal behavior and has visited some of the world's remotest places to track species such as gorillas, pandas and polar bears. Michael has filmed over 100 wildlife TV programs and written 28 books.

Meriel Lland teaches at Manchester Metropolitan University, UK. She is a writer, photographer and film-artist entranced by the stories we tell of the natural world and the secrets those stories reveal of their tellers. She's traveled with reindeer in Scandinavia, elephants in Africa and camels in Morocco. Meriel's writing and images have appeared in wildlife publications worldwide.

Michael and Meriel are passionate about conservation of the natural world and have worked with many global wildlife charities. For more information, see: www.michael-leach.co.uk and www.meriellland.co.uk

Acknowledgments

The publisher thanks the following agencies for their kind permission to use their images.
Key: t=top, b=bottom, l=left, r=right, c = center

Alamy Stock Photo 12/13 (main) Paul R. Sterry/ Nature Photographers Ltd, 14/15 © Stocktrek Images, Inc., 16/17 (main) © age fotostock, 16bl © National Geographic Creative, 26cl © David Chapman, 28cl © Andrew Harker, 31tr © blickwinkel, 32b tl © Pat Bennett, 33br © Zute Lightfoot, 34br © Marcus Harrison - outdoors, 46/47 © Nick Upton, 49c © Warwick Sloss, 57b © Leon Werdinger, 68/69 © parkerphotography, 71tr © Cultura RM, 72/73 © Design Pics Inc, 72bl © blickwinkel, 72br © blickwinkel, 82/83 © Mark J. Barrett, 85c © Jack Sullivan.

Corbis images 6/7 © Zero Creatives/cultura/ Corbis, 20/21 © Zero Creatives/cultura/Corbis, 26/27 © James Hager/robertharding/Corbis, 30/31 © Tim Laman/National Geographic Creative/Corbis, 44/45 © Martin Harvey/Corbis, 70/71 © Tobias Richter/Tobias Richter/Lookfoto/Corbis, 87tr © Roger Tidman/Corbis, 88/89 © Hero Images/Corbis, 90/91 © Colin Anderson/Blend Images/Corbis, 91tl © BERND WEISSBROD/epa/Corbis, 91c © Joel Sartore/National Geographic Creative/Corbis.

FLPA 32b tr Malcolm Schuyl/FLPA

Getty Images 4/5 Jeremy Woodhouse, 9tr Hero Images, 12bl PeopleImages, 58b Tim Ridley, 60/61 Adrian Weinbrecht.

Michael Leach and Meriel Lland 1tr, 1cr, 2br, 3t, 23tr, 23cl, 32br, 33tl 34tr x2, 34bl, 38b, 48t, 48b, 49t, 62t x2, 63b, 74tr x2, 74cr, 78br, 80/81b, 85b, 86t, 86b, 87bl, 87br.

Nature Picture Library 28/29 Klaus Echle, 32/33 Roland Seitre, 36/37 Sam Hobson, 46br Eric Medard, 50/51 ARCO / Kutschenreiter, 53cr t Ingo Arndt, 54/55 Florian Möllers, 56b Espen Bergersen, 59tl Juan Carlos Munoz, 64/65 Peter Cairns, 76/77 Klein & Hubert, 80/81 Visuals Unlimited.

www.aphotomarine.com 60ct (aquascope)

Photoshot 84b Photographer: Andrea and Antonella Ferrari

Shutterstock 1b Sparkling Moments Photography, 2-3 b/g Kichigin, 3b yurchello108, 5tr Steven Ward, 8bl Feng Yu, 8/9 soft_light, 10 Kletr, 10/11 b/g Dmitry_Tsvetkov, 11tr (x3 pics) estherpoon, 11 (main) KANIN.studio, 12/13 b/g Creative Travel Projects, 13tr l i g h t p o e t, 13cl Volodymyr Burdiak, 15tr (lying down) Leremy, 15tr (running man) file404, 15tr (footprints) mtmmarek, 15tr (perfume) DeCe, 15tr (necklace) Kapreski, 15tr (binocs) ekler, 15bl homydesign, 16/17 b/g Dhoxax, 17bl Pefkos, 17bc Africa Studio, 17br phatisakolpap, 18/19 Stephan Morris, 20c (a)

valleyboi63, 20c (b) bioraven, 20c (c) 3523studio, 20c (d) bioraven, 20c (e) Sigur, 21cl francesco de marco, 21cr kostin77, 22/23 Thomas Zsebok, 24/25 Medvedev Vladimir, 24cl Steve Allen, 25tr (squirrel) Lifeking, 25tr (fox) Airin.dizain, 25tr (badger) yyang, 29tr (deer) predragilievski, 30cr Michele Cozzolino, 30bl (branch) PinkPueblo, 30bl (man sitting) Satika, 32b bl Atmaji Widiyuswanto, 33tl Leremy, 34/35 b/g Sergieiev, 35tr Tom Tietz, 35b Kagai19927, 38/39 Mark Bridger, 38c (starling) Ozerov Alexander, 39tr lzf, 39cl Tony Moran, 39c Melinda Fawver, 39cr Robert Fowler, 39bl Andrey Shcherbukhin, 39bc dirkr, 39br Cosmin Coita, 40/41 alexkatkov, 41tl Leremy, 41bl jennyt, 42/43 Aleksey Stemmer, 43tr Dec Hogan, 44bl (ladybird) Yellowj, 44bc (lacewing) Jurik Peter, 45tr mborgali, 46bl Keith Bell, 47cr Erni, 48/49 b/g Jirat Teparaksa, 49b Piotr Kamionka, 52c (starfish) golubok, 52c (dolphin) Cjwhitewine, 52c (seal) Cattallina, 52c (dragonfly) agongallud, 52c (beaver) yyang, 52/53 Tory Kallman, 53c Adwo, 53cr b Jody Ann, 53b Vitalii Hulai, 54cr Roman Sotola, 54bc VoodooDot, 55cl Roman Sotola, 55cr Vector Market, 55bl Puckung, 56/57 Captiva55, 57t Matt Howard, 58/59 b/g padung, 58/59 David Osborn, 58c Wollertz, 59tr (gull) BillieBonsor, 59c (duck) Bennian, 59c (goose) Ina Raschke, 59c (coot) Nina B, 59b Volt Collection, 60c Joy Prescott, 60b Randimal, 61cl Heather Lucia Snow, 61cr Matthew Gough, 61bl Lori Froeb, 61br Marie Cloke, 62b FloridaStock, 63t Images By Kenny, 63cl omphoto, 66/67 Josh Schutz, 66tr Vladimir Kogan Michael, 66cl Chris Hill, 66cr Ben Queenborough, 66bl ueuaphoto, 66br Robert Asento, 67tr (kestrel) Vitaly Ilyasov, 67tl Aleksandr Sulga, 67cl (osprey) Gallinago_media, 67cl (falcon) yyang, 67cr Jessmine, 68bl Vitezslav Malina, 69tr (man) Leremy, 69tr (wind) Wiktoria Pawlak, 69tl moj0j0, 69cr Leremy, 70b Daxiao Productions, 73c James Tarver Photography, 74/75 SergeBertasiusPhotography, 74br tranac, 75cl Maria Dryfhout, 75cr Erwin Niemand, 75br Vitalii Nesterchuk, 78/79 sumikophoto, 78cl Laurent Renault, 78cr Soru Epotok, 78bl Inge Jansen, 78br iliuta goean, 79 l (top to bottom), a) (countryside) VoodooDot, d) (walking dog) Barry Barnes, e) (consider) Leremy, f) (livestock) vip2807, g) (protect) Epsicons, 79r (top to bottom), a) (fire) Liudmyla Marykon, b) (plan) SoleilC, c) (litter) davorana, d) (roads) microvector, e) (noise) graphic stocker, f) (signpost) SIM VA, g) (care) Kalabukhava Iryna, 80/81 b/g AwaylGl, 82bl bioraven, 82br Martial Red, 83bl eprom, 84/85 Erni, 86/87 b/g Alexander Lebedev, 90br (computer) fad82, 90br (panda) Birdiegal, 92/93 (girl) auremar, 92/93 (screen image) IanC66, 92cl think4photop, 92bl (book) irbis pictures, 92bl (image in book) TSpider, 93tr Alena Ozerova, 93tr AlexussK, 93cr Sarah Lew, 94/95 b/g Dr Ajay Kumar Singh, 95 Anton_Ivanov, 96 b/g Szczepan Klejbuk.

Illustrations: Unless otherwise stated, all illustrations © Marshall Editions.